The Hinds Family of Kent England

by Lorine McGinnis Schulze

ISBN: 978-1-987938-17-3
Publisher Olive Tree Genealogy

Over the last 40 plus years I have researched and gathered a great deal of information and uncovered many documents for my mother's ancestors in England. Pondering how best to preserve my research and share the stories of these maternal ancestors, I decided to compile books on each family surname.

Because the books were written for family, I have not cited my sources nor have I written long chapters of anecdotal stories. Instead I opted to create a chronological timeline for each generation. Images for all baptismal, marriage, burial, land records and so on that were discovered for each ancestor are also included.

If siblings were found, family group sheets are included. If they were not found, only my direct ancestor is noted. At the end of the book you will find blank pages for your own notes.

Those who want to know my sources can contact me directly through my website Olive Tree Genealogy at www.OliveTreeGenealogy.com My email is found at the bottom of each page.

I hope that readers enjoy these books and the stories of the ancestors.

Lorine McGinnis Schulze

Table of Contents

Hinds Family of Kent England

My Hinds ancestry has been found in Ramsgate Kent England as far back as Thomas Hinds born circa 1670. He may have been the son of John and Alice Hinds but proof is needed before we can claim this ancestry.

The surname has been found in original records as Hinds, Hynds, Hindes, Hyndes, Hind, Hynd, Hinde, and Hynde.

Spousal surnames include Ammos (Ammis?), Moses (Moyses), Ellington (Ellinton), Joad, Slaughter, Wood, Hubbard and Burbank.

Churches the families attended over the generations were St. Laurence (in Ramsgate), Ebenezer Chapel (in Ramsgate) and St. Paul's (in Canterbury).

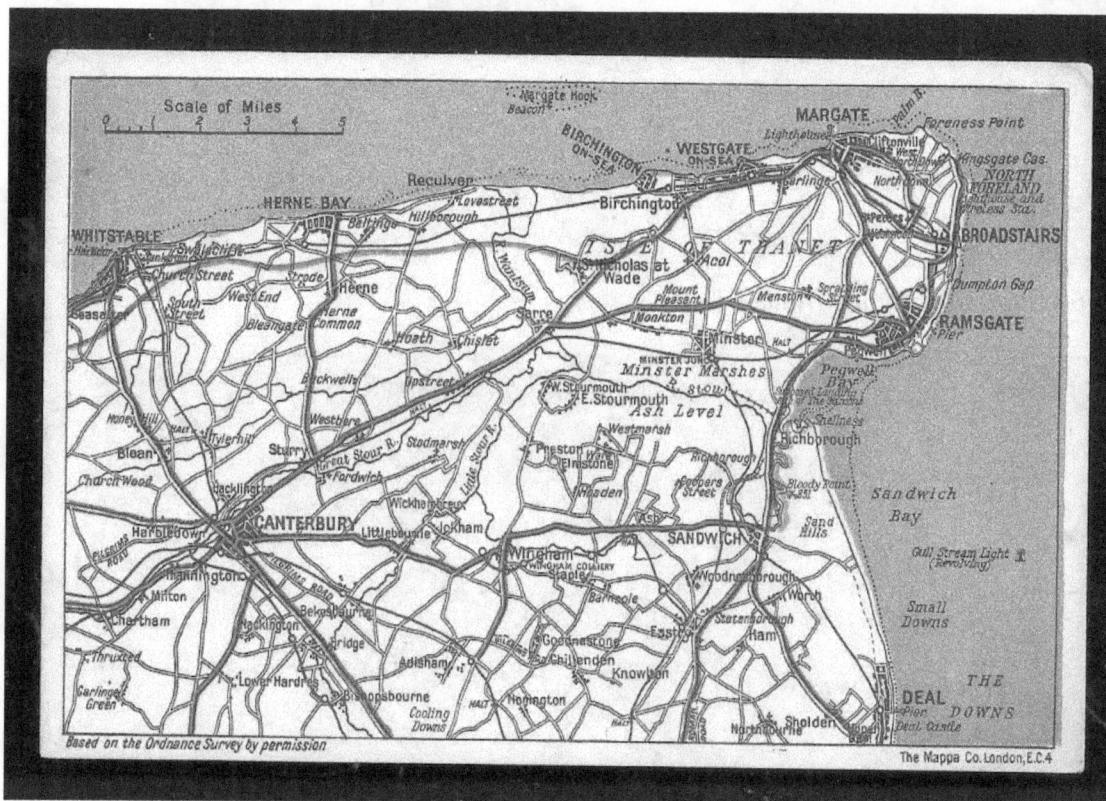

Postcard ca 1922 with map of Ramsgate and environs

Thomas Hinds ca 1670-1748 & Sarah Ammis

My 5th great-grandfather Thomas Hinds married Sarah Ammis on 19 February 1694 in St. Paul's, Canterbury England. Sarah was from St. Lawrence in Thanet, part of Ramsgate Kent. Sarah's age was given as 22 years. Thomas was recorded as a yeoman aged 23, from Woodnesborough. Woodnesborough is a village in East Kent two miles west of Sandwich. Its name is first attested in the Domesday Book of 1086 as Golles-Wanesberge.

There is a baptism for a Thomas Hinds in Sandwich on 25 February 1668 to John Hinds. We do not know if this is our Thomas but given the name of his firstborn son "John", it seems possible.

1668 Baptism Thomas Hinds

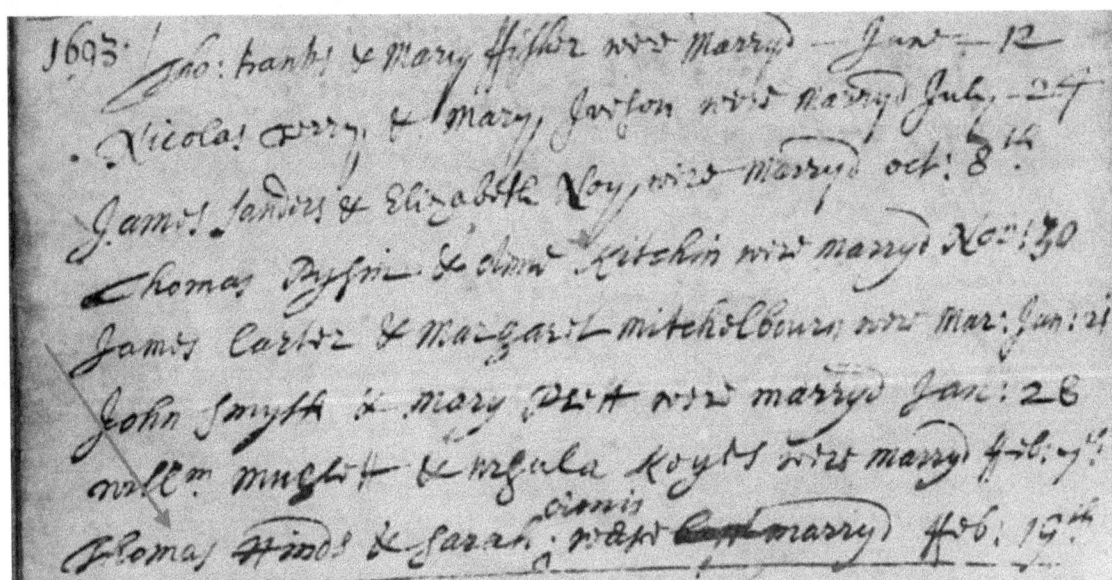

1693 Marriage Thomas & Sarah

Their seven known children (John 1697, William 1703, Sarah 1704, Mary 1705, Daniel 1708, Jeremiah 1711, and James 1713) were all baptised in Ebenezer Baptist Chapel in Ramsgate.

On 09 Nov 1744 Sarah was buried from St. Laurence in Thanet. Thomas Hind was buried St. Laurence in Thanet on 08 November 1748.

Burial Sarah Hind 1744

Burial Thomas Hind 1748

St.Laurence, Ramsgate

Family Group Sheet for Thomas Hinds

Husband:		Thomas Hinds
	b:	1670
	d:	1748 in St Lawrence in Thanet, St Lawrence Kent
	m:	19 Feb 1693 in Canterbury England
	Father:	John Hinds
	Mother:	Alice
Wife:		Sarah Annis or Dionas or Ammis
	b:	1671
	d:	09 Nov 1744 in St Lawrence in Thanet, St Lawrence Kent
	Father:	
	Mother:	
Children:		
1 M	Name: b:	John Hinds 02 May 1697 in Ramsgate, Ebenezer Chapel (Independent
2 M	Name: b:	William Hinds 24 Apr 1703 in Ramsgate, Ebenezer Chapel (Independent
3 F	Name: b:	Sarah Hinds 17 Mar 1704 in Ramsgate, Ebenezer Chapel (Independent
4 F	Name: b:	Mary Hinds 18 Jan 1706 in Ramsgate, Ebenezer Chapel (Independent
5 M	Name: b: d: m: Spouse:	Daniel Hinds 05 Mar 1708 in Ramsgate, Ebenezer Chapel (Independent 20 Jan 1793 in St Lawrence in Thanet, St Lawrence Kent 24 Dec 1730 Mary Moses
6 M	Name: b:	Jeremiah Hinds 24 Apr 1711 in Ramsgate, Ebenezer Chapel (Independent
7 M	Name: b:	James Hinds 22 May 1713 in Ramsgate, Ebenezer Chapel (Independent

Baptism William Hinds 1703

Baptism Sarah Hinds 1704

Baptism Mary Hinds 1706

Baptism Daniel Hinds 1708

Baptism Jeremiah Hinds 1711

Baptism James Hinds 1713

Daniel Hinds 1708-1793 & Mary Moses

My 7th great-grandfather Daniel, son of Thomas Hinds and Sarah Ammis, was born 05 March 1708 and baptised 16 March 1708 privately and the baptism registered in Ebenezer Baptist Chapel in Ramsgate Kent.

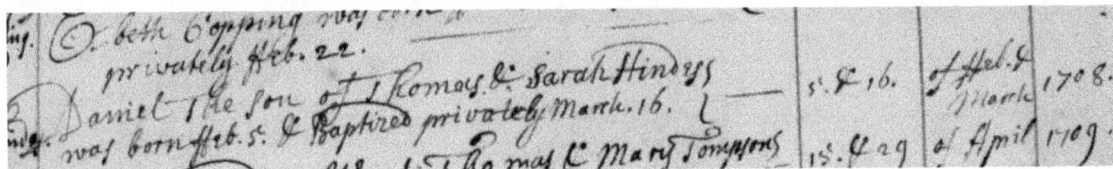

Later baptisms of other children have notations about the family's place of residence, but they are difficult to interpret. I include crops of each notation here for interested descendants to study.

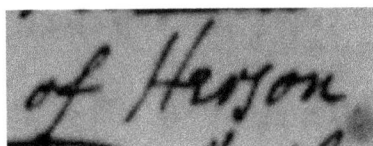

1703

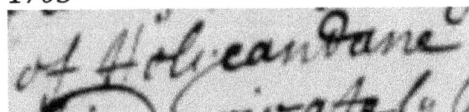

1713

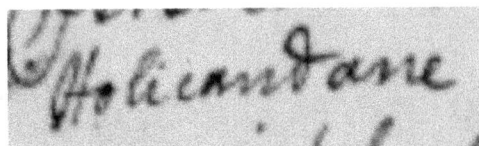

1711

Holiconbane is a street in Ramsgate, and I am fairly confident that this is where the family lived in 1711 and1713. Perhaps the notation was referring to where the private baptism took place.

On 24 Dec 1730 Daniel married Mary Moses in Thanet St Lawrence, Kent. She was baptised 08 February 1708 in St. Laurence in Thanet. Her parents wee recorded as John and Elizabeth Moses.

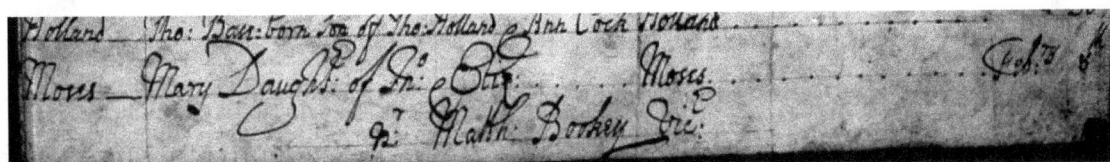

Baptism of Mary Moses 1708

We only find five children born to this couple: Elizabeth who was buried in St. Laurence in 1740 (no birth record found), John born 1735, Brooke born 1741, George born 1743, and another Elizabeth born 1746 died 1747.

Burial of Daniel Hinds 1793

Daniel was buried on 20 January 1703 from St. Laurence. Mary followed a few years later, dying of "decay" at the age of 93 and buried in the same church on 02 February 1802.

Burial of Mary Hinds 1802

Mary Hinds was interred in the church of St. Laurence in Ramsgate with her parents. Here is the inscription

*... on a slab covered by seats; surmounted by the following Coat of Arms for MOSES, gules, a chevron between three cocks heads or. Crest, a greyhound's head erased, regardant. "Here lieth ye body of Elizabeth, wife of Capt. John Moses, who died June ye 28th 1735 in ye 54th year of her age. And likewise hereunder lies ye body of Capt. John Moses, who died September the 22nd 1733 in ye 56 year of his age. They left issue two sons and three daughters, viz: John, George, Elizabeth, Ann, Mary. Here also lies ye body of Mr George Moses, son of ye above said John and Elizabeth Moses, who died October ye 16 1741 in ye 27 year of his age. **Also Mary HINDS, buried February 2 1802 aged 93 years.** Also John MOSES, nephwr (sic) of the said George Moses, who died July 7th 1817 aged 77 years."*

Family Group Sheet for Daniel Hinds

Husband:		Daniel Hinds
	b:	05 Mar 1708 in Ramsgate, Ebenezer Chapel (Independent
	d:	20 Jan 1793 in St Lawrence in Thanet, St Lawrence Kent
	m:	24 Dec 1730
	Father:	Thomas Hinds
	Mother:	Sarah Annis or Dionas or Ammis
Wife:		Mary Moses
	b:	08 Feb 1708 in St Lawrence in Thanet, St Lawrence Kent
	d:	02 Feb 1802
	Father:	John Moses
	Mother:	Elizabeth Brooke
Children:		
1 F	Name:	Elizabeth Hinds
	b:	Bet. 1731-1740
	d:	08 Aug 1740 in St Lawrence in Thanet, St Lawrence Kent
2 M	Name:	John Hinds
	b:	28 Feb 1735 in St Lawrence in Thanet, St Lawrence Kent
	d:	07 Apr 1768 in St Lawrence in Thanet, St Lawrence Kent
	m:	01 Jan 1763 in St Lawrence in Thanet, St Lawrence Kent
	Spouse:	Mildred Ellington
3 M	Name:	Brooke Hinds
	b:	08 Nov 1741 in St Lawrence in Thanet, St Lawrence Kent
	d:	15 Jun 1808 in St Lawrence in Thanet, St Lawrence Kent
	m:	11 Oct 1772 in St Lawrence in Thanet, St Lawrence Kent
	Spouse:	Sarah Joad
4 M	Name:	George Hinds
	b:	20 Nov 1743 in St Lawrence in Thanet, St Lawrence Kent
	m:	06 Jul 1773 in St Lawrence in Thanet, St Lawrence Kent
	Spouse:	Ann Wood
5 F	Name:	Elizabeth Hinds
	b:	19 Jan 1746 in St Lawrence in Thanet, St Lawrence Kent
	d:	02 Jan 1747 in St Lawrence in Thanet, St Lawrence Kent

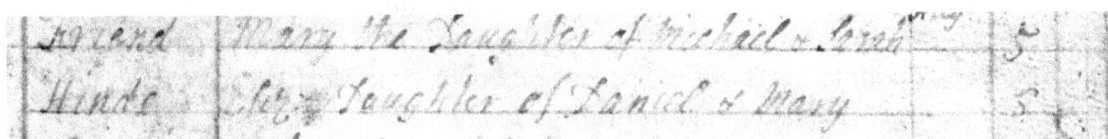

Death Elizabeth Hinds 1740

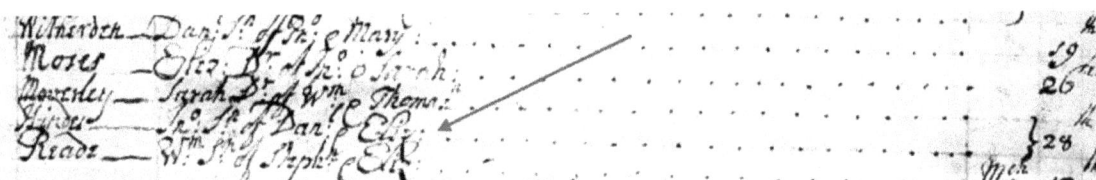

Baptism John Hinds 1735

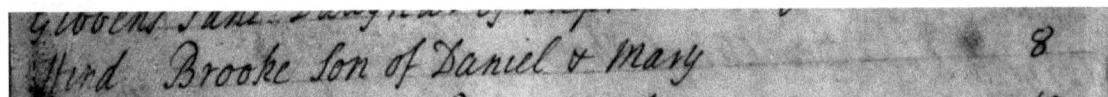

Baptism Brooke Hinds 1741

(The Year 1772)   Page 95

No 377

Brooke Hinds — — — — — — of [this] Parish, Batchelor — —
and Sarah Joad — — — — — — — — — of [this]
Parish, Spinster — — — — — — — — — — were
Married in this [Church] by [Lianse]
this eleventh — Day of October — in the Year One Thousand Seven Hundred
and Seventy two — — by me R Harvey [Vicar]
This Marriage was { Brooke Hinds
solemnized between Us { Sarah Joad
In the { Esther Joad
Presence of { Sarah Hinds

377 Hinds Brooke, Batchelor & Joad, Sarah, Spinster   Liano October 11

Marriage Brooke Hinds 1772

No 755 { Brooke Hinds — — — — — — — of this Parish
Widower and Mary Slaughter of this Parish Widow — — —
— — were
Married in this Church by License — — — — — —
this fourteenth Day of June in the Year One Thousand Seven Hundred
and eighty nine — — By me R Harvey Vicar
This Marriage was solemnized between Us { Brooke Hinds
{ Mary Slaughter
In the Presence of { John Hales
{ John Smith

Marriage Brooke Hinds 1789

Hales	Jane		Decay	77	Cy		15
Hinds	Brook		Mortification	67	Cy		15
Andews	William		Inflammation	37	Cy		21

Burial Brooke Hinds 1808

Elizabeth Daughter of Richard & Mary Jones
Sarah Daughter of William & Sarah Harlow } Nov 13
Mary Daughter of Parker & Mary East }
Hind George Son of Daniel & Mary   20

Baptism George Hinds 1743

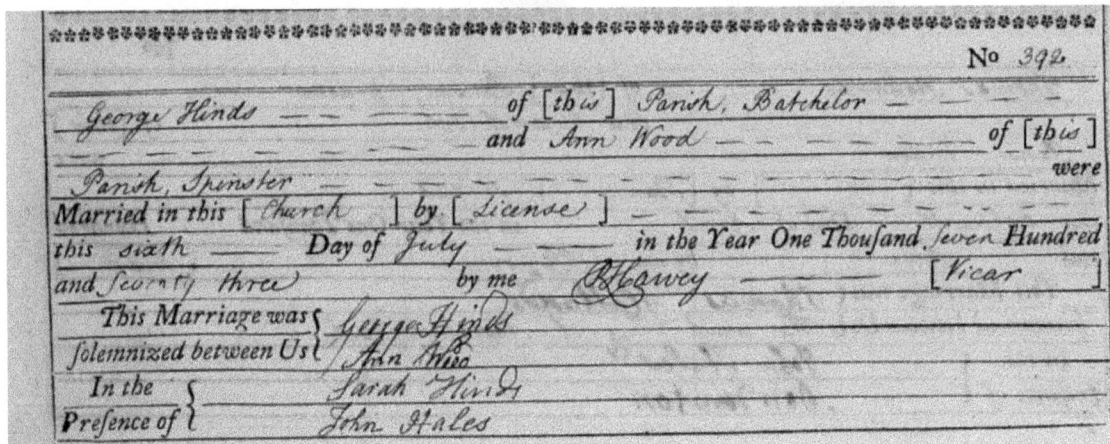

Marriage George Hinds 1773

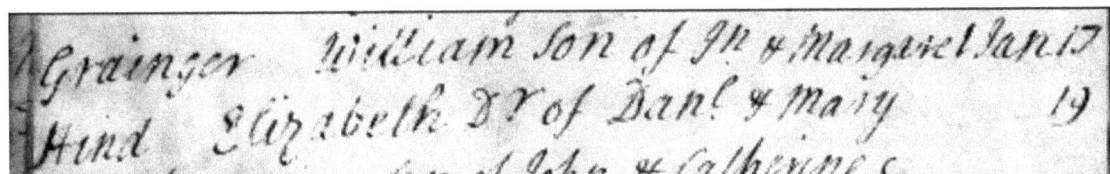

Baptism Elizabeth Hinds 1746

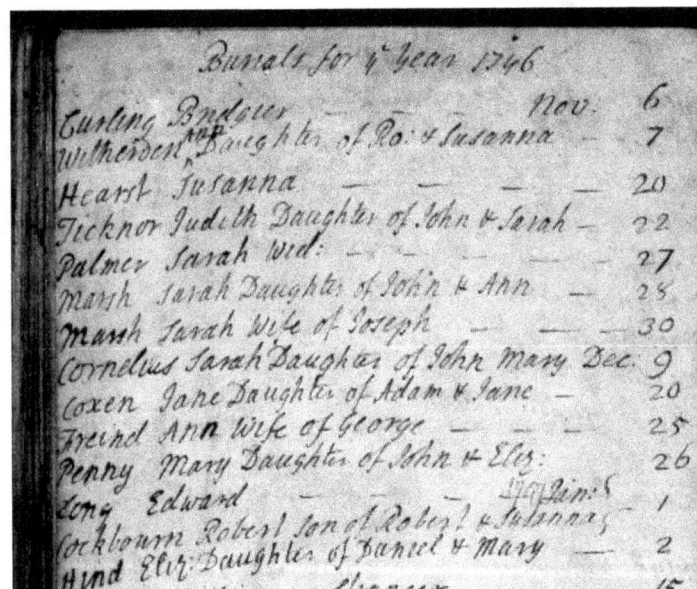

Burial Elizabeth Hinds 1747

John Hinds 1735-1768 & Mildred Ellington

My 6th great-grandfather John Hinds was baptised February 28, 1735 in St. Lawrence to Daniel and Elizabeth

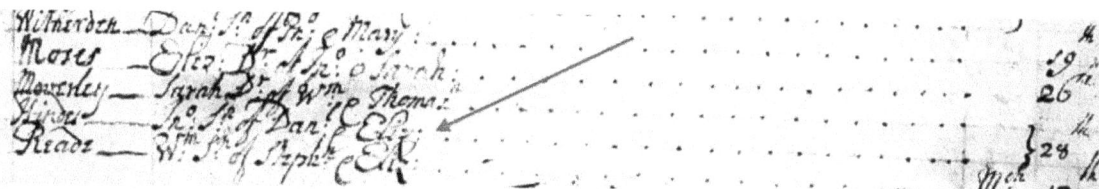

Baptism John 1735

On 01 Jan 1763 he married Mildred Ellington at St Lawrence in Thanet. Mildred was the daughter of Thomas and Sarah Ellington and was baptised in St. Lawrence on 20 November 1737.

They had two children baptised in St. Lawrence - Elizabeth Moses Hinds born 1764 and John Moses Hinds born 1765. In 1766 their toddler John Moses died and was buried at St. Lawrence. Two years later Mildred's husband died.

John Sr. died at age 33 and was buried 07 Apr 1768 from the church of St. Laurence. The original church register provides the ages of those who died, which is very unusual. But notice that the handwritten copy omits the ages which is a real shame. The age verifies that you have the right person and gives an estimated year of birth if you didn't know it.

Burial John 1768

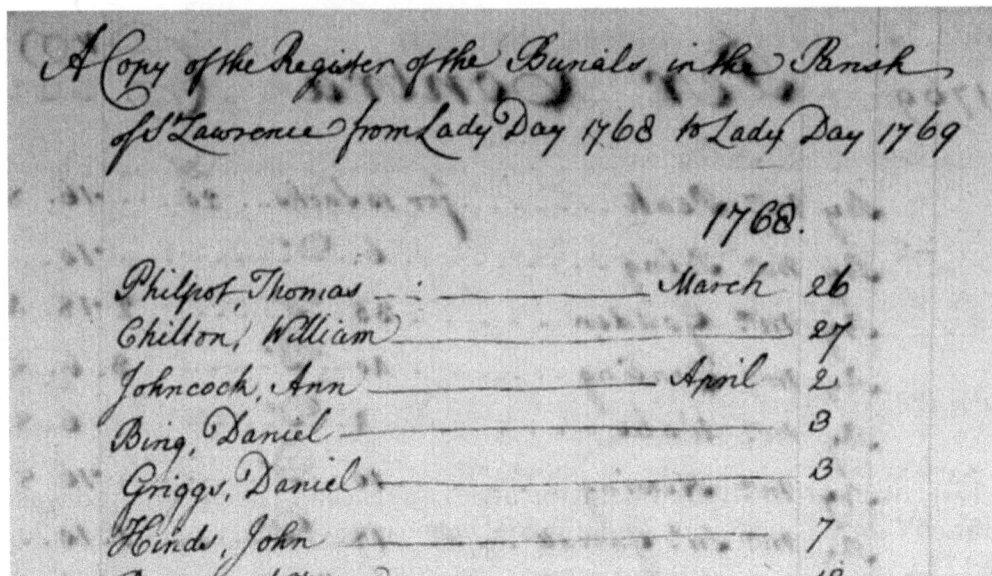

In 1769 his widow Mildred remarried to John Goss. Notice that she could write her own name so she may have been from a family with money.

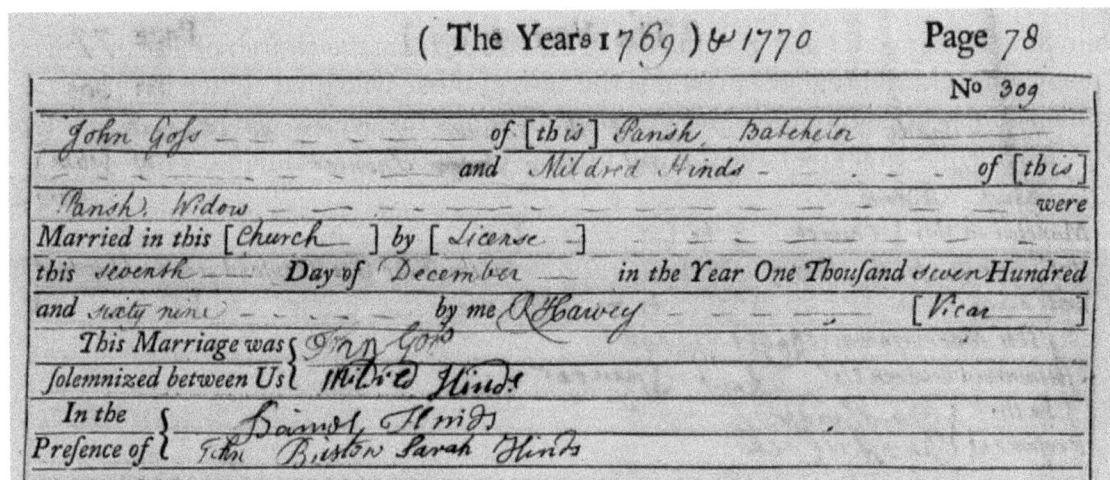

It appears that her father-in-law Daniel Hinds was one of the witnesses.

No children have been found for this marriage of Mildred and John Goss. Mildred died at the age of 79 and was buried on 12 January 1817 in St. Lawrence. She is noted as living in Ramsgate.

Page 64.

BURIALS in the Parish of *Lawrence in Thanet*
in the County of *Kent* in the Year 18*17*

Name.	Abode.	When buried.	Age.	By whom the Ceremony was performed.
Hoile Mary Ann No. 505.	Ramsgate	January 5	Infant	G. Abbot
Porter Samuel No. 506.	Bridge Town Glasgow	7	31	R. Harvey Jun!
Cox Mary. No. 507.	Margate	8	61	R. Harvey Jun!
Goff Mildred No. 508.	Ramsgate	12	79	G. Abbot
	Wife of Patrie			

Family Group Sheet for John Hinds

Husband:		John Hinds
	b:	28 Feb 1735 in St Lawrence in Thanet, St Lawrence Kent
	d:	07 Apr 1768 in St Lawrence in Thanet, St Lawrence Kent
	m:	01 Jan 1763 in St Lawrence in Thanet, St Lawrence Kent
	Father:	Daniel Hinds
	Mother:	Mary Moses
Wife:		Mildred Ellington
	b:	20 Nov 1737 in St Lawrence in Thanet, St Lawrence Kent
	d:	12 Jan 1817 in St Lawrence in Thanet, St Lawrence Kent
	Father:	Thomas Ellington
	Mother:	Sarah
Children:		
1 F	Name:	Elizabeth (Betsy) Moses Hinds
	b:	02 Feb 1764 in St Lawrence in Thanet, St Lawrence Kent
	m:	17 Oct 1787 in Saint Laurence, Thanet, Kent, Eng
	Spouse:	Philip Hubbard
2 M	Name:	John Moses Hinds
	b:	26 Aug 1765 in St Lawrence in Thanet, St Lawrence Kent
	d:	04 Mar 1766 in St Lawrence in Thanet, St Lawrence Kent

Elizabeth Moses Hinds 1764-? & 1. Richard Burbank 2. Philip Hubbard

My 5th great-grandmother Elizabeth Moses Hind(s) was baptised in St. Lawrence, Thanet Kent on February 2, 1764 to John and Mildred Hind(s)

Elizabeth married twice – first to Richard Burbank and secondly to my 5th great-grandfather Philip Hubbard.

Philip Hubbard, widower & Elizabeth Moses Burbank widow both of St. Laurence, Wit:
Philip Hubbard & John Goss

Further checking of church records showed that Betsy Moses married Richard
Burbank on 03 June 1785 in St. Laurence, Thanet, Kent.

In the register, Betsy is noted as Elizabeth Moses Hinds, spinster.

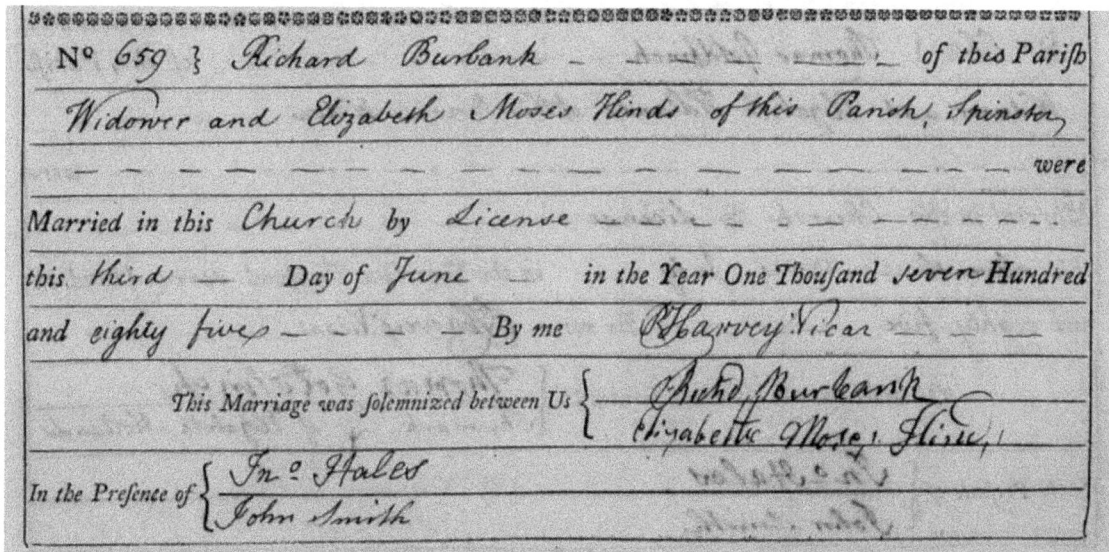

Richard Burbank made his will leaving most of his estate to his wife Elizabeth Moses
Burbank. It was proved 5th August 1775. He mentions that if he and Elizabeth have
children they are to receive a share. He also names his brother Robert Burbank,
sister Ann Parrot (?) widow, Elizabeth wife of Joseph Smith, and Mary wife of John
Stafford.

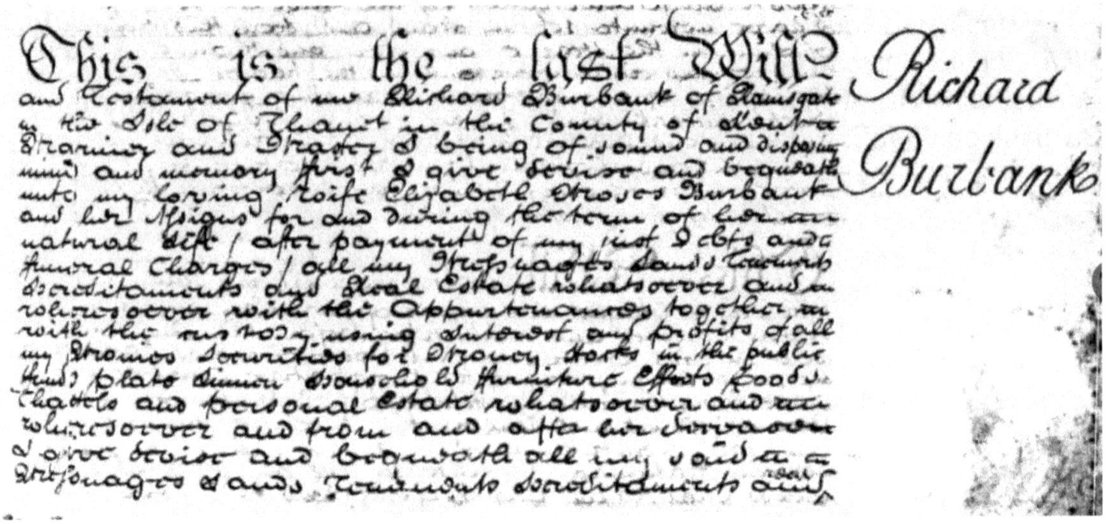

Estate with the appurtenances ~~~~~ ~~~~~ and all my said various securities for money & plate linnen & household furniture effects goods & chattels and personal Estate whatsoever to all and every my child and children as well such as shall be born before my decease as after equally to be divided between such children if more than one and they to take a take as Tenants in common and not as joint Tenants but if I shall leave no such child or children or if I shall leave any such child or children all such children shall happen to die under the age of twenty one years without leaving any lawful Issue of his her or their Bodies lawfully then I give devise and bequeath all my said Messuages Lands Tenements hereditaments and Real Estate and the Dividends Interest and profits of all my said various securities for money Effects Goods Chattels and personal Estate to my Brother and Sisters Robert Burbank Ann Barrett Widow Elizabeth wife of Joseph Smith and Mary wife of John Stafford for and during the term of their respective natural lives and from and after their decease respectively I give devise and bequeath the same Messuages Lands Tenements Monies Securities and my said Real and personal Estate to all and every the child and children of my said Brother and Sister Robert Burbank and Ann Barrett equally to be divided between them share and share alike and to their respective heirs Executors Administrators and Assigns to hold the same as Tenants in common and not as joint Tenants And I appoint my said Wife sole Executrix of this my last Will and Testament and do hereby revoke all former Wills by me made In witness whereof I have hereunto set my hand and seal this eighth day of June in the year of our said one thousand seven hundred and eighty five and in the twenty fifth year of the Reign of our sovereign lord King George the third &c Rich.d Burbank (Seal) signed sealed published and declared by the said Richard Burbank the Testator as and for his last Will and Testament in the presence of us who have subscribed our names in his present Richard Peter Pilcher Longley, John Daniel

𝕿𝖍𝖎𝖘 𝖂𝖎𝖑𝖑 was proved at London the twenty fifth day of August in the year of our Lord one thousand seven hundred and eighty five before the Right or a a Worshipful peter Calvert Doctor of Laws Master or Keeper or Commissary of the prerogative Court of a a a Canterbury lawfully constituted by the oath of Elizabeth various Burbank widow the Relict of the deceased and sole Executrix named in the said Will to whom Administration was granted of all and singular the goods Chattels and Credits of the said deceased she

she having been first sworn by commission duly to administer

Family Group Sheet for Elizabeth (Betsy) Moses Hinds

Husband:		Philip Hubbard
	b:	08 Jan 1753 in Dover, Kent England
	m:	17 Oct 1787 in Saint Laurence, Thanet, Kent, Eng
	Father:	Philip Hubbard
	Mother:	Emblen Smithett
Wife:		Elizabeth (Betsy) Moses Hinds
	b:	02 Feb 1764 in St Lawrence in Thanet, St Lawrence Kent
	Father:	John Hinds
	Mother:	Mildred Ellington
Children:		
1 F	Name:	Milly Elizabeth Hubbard
	b:	27 Jul 1788 in Saint Laurence, Thanet, Kent, Eng
	d:	13 May 1871 in Ramsgate, Kent Eng
	m:	06 Jun 1805 in St. Laurence, Ramsgate, Kent Eng.
	Spouse:	John Caspall
2 F	Name:	Margaret Hubbard
	b:	28 Jan 1790 in Saint Laurence, Thanet, Kent, Eng
	m:	23 May 1807
	Spouse:	Samuel Bailey
3 F	Name:	Elizabeth Hubbard
	b:	12 Oct 1791 in Saint Laurence, Thanet, Kent, Eng
	d:	Dec 1792 in Saint Laurence, Thanet, Kent, Eng
4 F	Name:	Elizabeth Hubbard
	b:	05 Nov 1792 in Saint Laurence, Thanet, Kent, Eng
5 F	Name:	Mary Ann Hubbard
	b:	24 Jun 1795 in Saint Laurence, Thanet, Kent, Eng
	m:	22 Jun 1820 in St Lawrence in Thanet, St Lawrence Kent
	Spouse:	John Packer

Notes